The Maya

by Petra Press

Content Adviser: Professor Sherry L. Field,
Department of Social Science Education, College of Education,
The University of Georgia

Reading Adviser: Dr. Linda D. Labbo,
Department of Reading Education, College of Education,
The University of Georgia

COMPASS POINT BOOKS

Minneapolis, Minnesota

FIRST REPORTS

Compass Point Books
3722 West 50th Street, #115
Minneapolis, MN 55410

Visit Compass Point Books on the Internet at *www.compasspointbooks.com* or e-mail your request to *custserv@compasspointbooks.com*

Front cover: Guatemalan bird-shaped pottery from A.D. 500

Photographs ©: Denver Art Museum 2001 (Bird-form vessel, ca. 500 A.D., Guatemala, Denver Art Museum Collection, Gift of Dr. & Mrs. M. Larry Ottis, 1991.659ab), cover; Unicorn Stock Photos/Jeff Greenberg, 4, 9 top; Photo Network/Jeff Greenberg, 5; XNR Productions, Inc., 6; TRIP/G. Howe, 7; Inga Spence/Visuals Unlimited, 8, 14, 36; Norris Blake/Visuals Unlimited, 9 bottom; Graeme Teague, 10, 13, 18, 19, 20, 42; Photo Network/Andrea Esty 12; David L. Brown/Tom Stack & Associates, 15, 32, 35, 39; Robert Fried/Tom Stack & Associates, 16; Unicorn Stock Photos/A. Ramey, 17; North Wind Picture Archives, 21, 23, 26, 29, 30; Archive Photos, 22, 40; Hulton Getty/Archive Photos, 24, 25; Stock Montage, 27; Unicorn Stock Photos/Bob Barrett, 28; Kjell Sandved/Visuals Unlimited, 31; Hulton Getty/Archive Photos, 33; Photo Network/Larry Dunmire, 34; Brian Parker/Tom Stack & Associates, 37; The Newberry Library/Stock Montage, 38; Reuters/Kimberly White/Archive Photos, 43.

Editors: E. Russell Primm, Emily J. Dolbear, and Alice K. Flanagan
Photo Researcher: Svetlana Zhurkina
Photo Selector: Catherine Neitge
Designer: Bradfordesign, Inc.

Library of Congress Cataloging-in-Publication Data
Press, Petra.
    The Maya / by Petra Press.
        p. cm. — (First reports)
    Includes bibliographical references and index.
    ISBN 0-7565-0081-8 (hardcover : lib. bdg.)
    1. Mayas—History—Juvenile literature. 2. Mayas—Social life and customs—Juvenile literature. [1. Mayas. 2. Indians of Central America.] I. Title. II. Series.
F1435 .P74 2001
972.81'016—dc21   00-011281

Table of Contents

Once a Great Nation

▲ *Guatemalan dancers wear Maya masks.*

The Maya (pronounced MYE-uh) are people called Mesoamericans. *Meso* is a Greek word meaning "middle."

Long ago the Maya lived in large cities in middle or Central America. They lived in the mountains and rain forests of what are now Guatemala, Honduras, and El Salvador. They also lived in northern Belize and parts of southern Mexico. Today's Maya live in the same areas, but the large cities are gone.

From A.D. 300 to 800, the Maya were a great nation. They were farmers and traders. They were talented builders too. At one time, they had more than 100 cities. They were known for their beautiful **pyramids** and temples.

▲ *The remains of a Maya temple in Mexico*

▲ A map of Maya lands

Then people began to leave the cities. It is not clear why. By about 900, most Maya had moved to other places.

Farming

The Maya have been farmers for more than 1,500 years. Their way of farming is very old. It is called slash-and-burn farming. First, the farmers rip off, or slash, the bark from trees in the rain forest. After the trees dry out, the farmers burn them to clear the land. Then they plant their seeds.

▲ *Maya farmers have practiced slash-and-burn farming for many years.*

In the past, the Maya planted corn, beans, squash, and chili peppers. Farmers also grew pineapples, papayas, and cacao. They made chocolate from cacao.

Corn, or maize, was their most important crop. The Maya called it "the sunbeam of the gods."

Maya farmers farmed the land in clever ways. They cut deep steps into the hills. Then they planted crops on the steps. When it rained, the crops did not wash

▲ Corn, or maize, was called "the sunbeam of the gods."

away. This is called terrace farming.

Every year, Maya farmers planted different crops in their fields. They changed what they grew. Changing the crops keeps the soil healthy.

◄ Maya women cook traditional food in Honduras.

▲ Corn is still the most important crop in Guatemala.

▲ *The Maya built homes by tying poles together.*

Living a Simple Life

Maya farmers lived in small villages near their fields. They built houses by tying poles together. They used palm leaves to make roofs.

In the village, everyone helped with the work. The men and older boys cleared the fields for farming. They also planted the seeds. They hunted and fished too.

The women and older girls made the clothing. They also cooked the meals. The Maya ate rabbit, deer, and turkey stews. The women also used corn to make flat cakes and bread. Today this kind of bread is called a tortilla.

When the Maya were not working, they made many useful things. Some of these things were very beautiful.

The men made stone tools. They also made tiny clay figures and jewelry from a green stone called jade. They wove ropes, baskets, and mats from different plants. The women made clay jars and pots. They painted them with pretty designs.

▲ *A Guatemalan woman weaves colorful designs.*

Trading

▲ *Canoes in Honduras*

As the villages grew, farmers began to trade the things they had made. Soon, roads led from village to village. In time, the roads also led to busy city markets.

The Maya had no horses or mules to carry their goods. They had to carry everything on their backs in backpacks. Many traders used a sling that hung from a strap across their forehead or chest. This kind of backpack is called a **tumpline**.

Some traders were lucky. They traveled along the coast or upriver by canoe.

The Maya traded their goods with others. Most traders wanted cacao beans, which were used as a kind of money. Many traders traded salt, animal furs, cloth, tools, and weapons for the beans. They also traded colorful bird feathers and stones.

Some Maya stole goods from neighboring villages. Soon, people wanted to defend themselves.

▲ *The inside of a cacao pod*

▲ *The remains of a Maya building in Chichén Itzá in Mexico*

They built walls around their villages. Before long, the strongest villages grew into great cities. Most traders set up markets in these cities. In time, the traders became rich and powerful.

▲ Chichén Itzá was a large Maya city in what is now the Yucatan in Mexico.

City Life

After many years, Maya cities became important trading centers. The largest cities were Tikal, Chichén Itzá, and Palenque. Between 30,000 and 60,000 people may have lived in these cities at one time.

Each city had its own way of speaking the Maya language. Each city had its own crafts and ways of life.

▲ *The remains of Tikal, in what is now Guatemala*

Thousands of buildings made up the large cities. There were pyramids, temples, palaces, and ballparks. The Maya made many man-made lakes too.

Workers cut the stone for the buildings from nearby **quarries**. They had to dig deep in the earth to find a quarry. Workers cut the stone into large blocks.

▲ *Grass has covered an old quarry in Honduras.*

▲ A piece of Maya pottery from the Yucatan in Mexico

Then they carried the blocks up the steep sides of the quarry and lifted them into place. Some Maya buildings were more than 200 feet (60 meters) high.

Cities were busy places. Wealthy traders sold their goods there. Priests performed **ceremonies**. A different king ruled each city. The larger cities governed the smaller cities around them.

The rich and powerful people were called noblemen. Sometimes, their families ruled the cities for hundreds of years. But it was the hardworking farmers and slaves who gave them their way of life.

The Upper Class

▲ *Murals decorated temples and homes.*

Noblemen were part of the upper class. They lived in large houses. In the houses were large wall paintings called **murals**.

Noblemen wore colorful clothing decorated with **embroidery**. Embroidery is the art of sewing pictures

▲ *Noblemen wore decorated headdresses.*

or designs onto cloth. Noblemen wore white cotton underclothes. They were embroidered and trimmed with feathers. On top of the underclothes, a nobleman wore a cotton robe made from animal skins.

He also wore a headdress made of colorful feathers from tropical birds. Sometimes the headdress was as long as the person was tall!

Women wore more simple clothing. They

▲ A Maya vase found in Mexico shows a man wearing a headdress with a jaguar on it.

dressed in loose cotton robes that they decorated with colorful embroidery.

The upper class had exact ideas about what made a person beautiful. They thought flat, sloping foreheads were very pretty. So parents flattened their baby's head. They pressed the baby's forehead with wooden boards for several days.

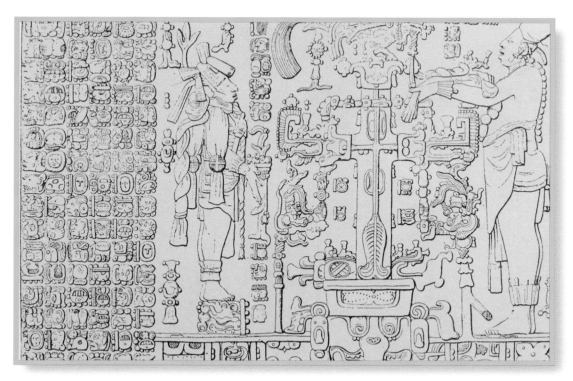

▲ *The figures on this tablet from a temple in Palenque have sloping foreheads.*

Men made their noses look like a bird's beak. They pierced their ears. And they glued green jade to their teeth. Many women filed their teeth into points.

▲ *A Maya nobleman with his slaves*

The Lower Class

Maya farmers were members of the lower class. They had to give two-thirds of their crops to the upper class. They worked hard for the upper class too. Men of the lower class wore plain cotton underclothes and simple clothes on top.

Women wore cotton blouses and skirts. Some wore loose-fitting dresses with simple embroidery. Women and girls wore their hair long. It was always combed neatly.

◀ *A Maya woman in the Yucatan wears an embroidered dress.*

▲ *Slaves hauled stones for building projects, such as the Palenque Palace.*

Slaves were the poorest people. They had very hard lives. Many hauled stones from quarries for building projects. They also worked in their owner's house. When the owners died, slaves were often killed. They were buried with their owners. People believed their slaves could serve them in the after-life.

Some people were born into slavery. Others became slaves when they broke the law or were taken prisoner in war. People bought and sold slaves in markets or traded them.

▲ *The "Tablet of the Slaves" is from a building in Palenque.*

Art and Science

The Maya made some of the most beautiful **sculptures**, buildings, and pottery in the world. They built great limestone pyramids and temples.

They also built houses for kings and noblemen.

▲ *The remains of the Court of 1,000 Columns in Chichén Itzá*

▲ *The Maya built beautiful palaces.*

Sculptors made pottery and statues to decorate buildings. Artists painted murals on the walls.

The Maya had a kind of writing called **hieroglyphics**. Only some Maya knew how to write. They were called **scribes**. They painted hieroglyphs in paper books. The paper was made from the inner bark of wild fig trees.

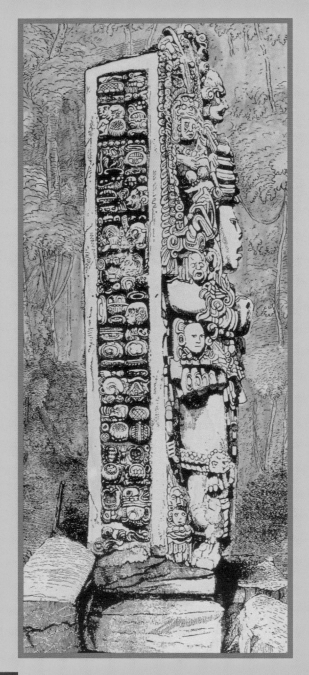

Scribes made calendars showing the best days for farming and hunting. Scribes also carved hieroglyphs on stone and wood. They recorded important dates and events on large stone monuments. We have some of these carvings today. They tell us a lot about the Maya.

The Maya were good at math. Many believe the Maya were the first to use the idea of zero.

◄ Scribes carved hieroglyphs on stone.

▲ *A Maya carving*

The Maya were also good at astronomy. Astronomy is the study of the stars, the planets, and space.

▲ *The Maya studied the stars and planets from this building in Chichén Itzá.*

▲ *A Maya calendar column*

The Maya followed the movements of the sun, the moon, and the stars very carefully. They knew when the moon would cover the sun in the sky. And they knew the best time to plant crops. Then they made calendars based on what they saw. In some ways, the Maya calendar was more useful than today's calendars.

Religion

Religion was important in Maya daily life. From morning to night, the Maya prayed to many gods. Some gods were helpful and some were harmful.

The main Maya god was Hunab Ku. The Maya believed that he created the world. Itzamna was the

▲ *Stone carvings decorate many Maya buildings.*

▲ *A statue of a Maya god in Chichén Itzá*

god of the heavens. He gave the Maya day and night. Yum Kaax was the corn god. The four Chacs were rain gods. Each was the god of a different direction and color of rain.

Women prayed to Ix Chel, the god of rainbows. A woman who needed help healing, giving birth, or

▲ *The remains of the temple in Tikal, Guatemala*

weaving prayed to this god.

To please the gods, the Maya held ceremonies in special temples. They gave gifts of corn, fruit, and meat to the gods. They also killed animals to feed the gods. Some people gave their own blood or the blood of others. Sometimes people were killed for the gods.

▲ *A Maya dancer performs in Mexico.*

The priests were in charge of the ceremonies. They had ceremonies to bury the dead and to honor a king. They also had special ceremonies for each month of the year and the new year. During these times, the people decorated their bodies with paint, feathers, and bells. They danced to the music of rattles, flutes, and drums.

Leaving the Cities

▲ *A monument at Copan, a Maya city in what is now Honduras*

From A.D. 300 to 800, as many as 14 million people may have lived in the Maya cities. After 800, many people began leaving the cities. They stopped building temples and palaces. And they no longer set up monuments to honor their gods.

Some people think that the Maya left the cities because there were too many wars. Others believe that a lack of water destroyed their crops. When they could not grow enough food to feed everyone, they moved away. The Maya in each city may have had a different reason for leaving.

After 900, a few cities in the Yucatan—Chichén Itzá, Uxmal, and Mayapán—began to grow again. But they were never as big as they had been.

▲ *The Pyramid of the Magician in Uxmal, Mexico*

▲ *Pedro de Alvarado was a Spanish conquistador who conquered the Maya.*

The Spaniards

In the early 1500s, soldiers came to the Americas from Spain. They came to explore the land. The soldiers also came to take gold and other riches back to Spain.

These Spanish soldiers were called **conquistadors**. In Spanish, *conquistador* means "conqueror."

The conquistadors did not care about the Maya people. They did not care about the Maya way of life. They destroyed many villages and made slaves of the people.

For a long time, the Maya fought the conquistadors. But then they lost their strength.

The Maya had very little food left. They got sick from the soldiers' strange illnesses. Many Maya died. By 1541, the Spaniards ruled most of Mexico and Central America.

The Maya Today

▲ *Farmers load dried crops on a truck in Honduras.*

Today, many people in Mexico and Central America
are related to the Maya. In Guatemala, more than half
of the people are Maya or **mestizo**. That means they
are part Spanish and part Maya. They speak a mixture
of Spanish and the Maya language.

Many Maya are farmers. They work the land in

much the same way as their relatives did long ago. Most Maya farmers are poor. Their houses do not have electricity. The people do not have doctors. And there are few schools for the children. But they are working to make life better.

The Maya are trying to save their language and traditions. They also want to make a bright future for their children. The Maya are proud of their culture and their great past.

▲ *Holding candles during a Maya ceremony in Guatemala*

Glossary

ceremonies—formal actions to mark important times

conquistadors—Spanish military leaders sent to take over Mexico, Central America, and South America

embroidery—the art of sewing designs onto cloth

hieroglyphics—a kind of writing that uses symbols and pictures to record events

mestizo—a person who is part European and part Native American; a mestizo in Guatemala is usually part Spanish and part Maya

murals—wall paintings

pyramids—buildings with a square base and four triangular sides

quarries—places where stone is dug from the ground

scribes—people who write information by hand

sculptures—images carved in wood or stone

tumpline—a sling that hangs from a strap across the forehead or chest to carry heavy loads

Did You Know?

- The Maya decorated their bodies with tattoos and paint. Rich people used red paint. Warriors used red and black. Priests painted themselves blue. Prisoners were painted with black and white stripes.

- The holy book of the Maya is called the *Popol Vuh*. It tells how the gods formed the world. Then they made people out of corn.

- The Maya did not always eat corn. At first, they made a drink from corn. Later, when the Maya learned how to grow larger cobs of corn, they began to eat it.

- The Maya kept dogs as pets.

At a Glance

Tribal name: Maya

Past locations: Northern Belize, El Salvador, Guatemala, Honduras, southern Mexico

Present locations: Northern Belize, El Salvador, Guatemala, Honduras, southern Mexico

Traditional houses: Pole-and-thatch houses, stone

Traditional clothing materials: Cotton, feathers, animal skins

Traditional transportation: Foot, dugout canoes

Traditional food: Corn, beans, chili peppers, papayas, pineapples, squash, tortillas, deer, rabbit, turkey

Important Dates

500 B.C.–1 B.C.	Maya cities develop.
350 B.C.–A.D. 30	The Maya invent a calendar and a form of writing.
A.D. 1–500	The Maya way of life spreads to other people.
300–800	The Maya are a great nation.
800–900	People leave the Maya cities.
1500s	Spanish explorers come to the Americas.
1541	Spaniards rule most of Mexico and Central America.
1800s	Mexico and Central America win their freedom from Spain.
1800–today	Mexico and Central America govern the Maya.

Want to Know More?

At the Library
Greene, Jacqueline D. *The Maya*. New York: Franklin Watts, 1992.
Nicholson, Robert. *The Maya*. New York: Chelsea House Press (Junior), 1994.
Sherrow, Victoria. *The Maya Indians*. New York: Chelsea House Publishers, 1994.

On the Web
Maya Discovery
http://www.mayadiscovery.com/ing/history/history.html
For information about Maya traders

Maya Adventure
http://www.sci.mus.mn.us/sin/ma/top.html
For science activities and information about ancient and modern Maya

Through the Mail
U Mut Maya
P.O. Box 4686
Arcata, CA 95518
To order a Maya hieroglyphic workbook

On the Road
The Minneapolis Institute of Arts
2400 Third Avenue South
Minneapolis, MN 55404
612/870-3200
To see Maya artifacts

Index

About the Author

Petra Press is a freelance writer of young adult nonfiction, specializing in the diverse culture of the Americas. Her more than twenty books include histories of U.S. immigration, education, and settlement of the West, as well as portraits of numerous indigenous cultures. She lives in Milwaukee, Wisconsin, with her husband, David.